LATER

Philip Gross was born in 1952 in Delabole, Cornwall. Professor of Creative Writing at the University of South Wales, he has taught writing at every step on the educational ladder from nursery to PhD, and relishes collaboration with musicians, dancers and visual artists of all kinds. A Quaker who has also written horror and science fiction, children's opera and radio plays, he now lives with his wife Zélie in Penarth in South Wales.

Since winning a Gregory Award in 1981 and first prize in the National Poetry Competition in 1982 he has published books with Peterloo, Faber and Bloodaxe, including *The Air Mines of Mistila*, with Sylvia Kantaris (1988: Poetry Book Society Choice) and *The Wasting Game* (1998: shortlisted for the Whitbread Poetry Award). Poems from all these and several small-press collections are brought together in *Changes of Address: Poems 1980-1998* (Bloodaxe Books, 2001). His later books include *Later* (2013); *Deep Field* (2011), a Poetry Book Society Recommendation, shortlisted for the Roland Mathias Poetry Award (Wales Book of the Year); *The Water Table* (2009), winner of the T.S. Eliot Prize; *The Egg of Zero* (2006); and *Mappa Mundi* (2003), a Poetry Book Society Recommendation – all from Bloodaxe – and *I Spy Pinhole Eye* (Cinnamon Press, 2009), in collaboration with photographer Simon Denison, which won the Wales Book of the Year Award 2010.

His poetry for children includes *Manifold Manor*, *The All-Nite Café* (winner of the Signal Award 1994), *Scratch City* and *Off Road To Everywhere* (winner of the CLPE Award 2011). Since *The Song of Gail and Fludd* (1991) he has published nine more novels for young people, most recently *The Storm Garden* (2006).

PHILIP GROSS

LATER

BLOODAXE BOOKS

Copyright © Philip Gross 2013

ISBN: 978 1 85224 979 3

First published 2013 by
Bloodaxe Books Ltd,
Highgreen,
Tarset,
Northumberland NE48 1RP.

www.bloodaxebooks.com
For further information about Bloodaxe titles
please visit our website or write to
the above address for a catalogue.

Supported by
**ARTS COUNCIL
ENGLAND**

Cover design: Neil Astley & Pamela Robertson-Pearce.

Printed in Great Britain by Bell & Bain Limited, Glasgow, Scotland, on
acid-free paper sourced from mills with FSC chain of custody certification.

It is worth pausing over the delicately shifting meanings of the word *late*, ranging from missed appointments through the cycles of nature to vanished life. Most frequently *late* just means 'too late', later than we should be, not on time. But late evenings, late blossoms, and late autumns are perfectly punctual – there isn't another clock or calendar they are supposed to match. Dead persons have certainly got themselves beyond time, but then what temporal longing lurks in our calling them 'late'? Lateness doesn't name a single relation to time, but it always brings time in its wake. It is a way of remembering time, whether it is missed or met or gone.

MICHAEL WOOD, introduction to Edward Said's *On Late Style*

ACKNOWLEDGEMENTS

Acknowledgments are due to the editors of the following publications in which some of these poems first appeared: *The Absent Photographer* (ed. Katy Giebenhain, photographs Stephanie Gibson, Middle Street, 2009), *The Best British Poetry 2011* and *2013* (ed. Roddy Lumsden, Salt), *Calon, Canto, Creative Writing: New Signals, New Territories* (American, British and Canadian Studies, Academic Anglophone Society of Romania), *Days of Roses, English, Estonian Literary Magazine, Friends Quarterly, The Guardian, The Ice Road* (Tallinn University, 2011), *Jubilee Lines* (ed. Carol Ann Duffy, Faber, 2012), *The Laurel Crown* (ed. with photographs, Jemimah Kuhfeld), *The London Magazine, Magma, Manhattan Review, New Welsh Review, Planet, Poetry and Audience, Poetry London, Poetry Review, Tokens for the Foundlings* (ed. Tony Curtis, Seren, 2011).

'Birch, His Book' appeared as a limited edition broadsheet from Mulfran Press, 2011, with original engraving by Jonathan Gross.

'Dirac: the Tower' owes its existence to Simon Thomas' sculpture 'Small Worlds'.

'Words for the Shortest Day' is printed and its genesis explored in 'Then Again What Do I Know: reflections on reflection in Creative Writing' in *The Writer in the Academy: Creative Interfrictions* (ed. R. Marggraf Turley, English Association, 2011).

The following poems first appeared with personal dedications: 'Barn Music', *for the Resonabilis ensemble, St Donat's and Tallinn, 2010*; 'Epiphany Weather', *for Petra and Jonathan*; 'Flying Down Wales', *for Gillian Clarke*; 'Legacy', *for Rosemary and Jonathan*; 'Orrery', *for Jonathan, at 30*; 'Spoor', thanks are due to Tsead Bruinja and Alexis Nouss; 'The Point', *for the Ice Road group, Tallinn*; 'The Works', *for Katy Giebenhain and Stephanie Gibson*; 'Whit', *for Jeremy Hooker*.

Many poems, of course, for John Karl Gross, *d.* 2011, and all with thanks to Zélie for a keen eye and love and support.

CONTENTS

Flying Down Wales

The wind bucks
but it doesn't refuse us
– does us no favours either,
no more than it would a moderately
                                successful bird.
The land, though, gives little away

from bird height.
(Swans, calmly rowing,
aren't unknown at 20,000 feet.)
Not dark yet, but the edges of things
                                begin to blur
as age will loosen our grip first on names,

nouns, days,
then on all definition...
We track down the knobble-
back spine of a difficult country –
                                surly wrinkles
in the grey, the sun withheld, till all at once

and suddenly
every tarn, stream-
capillary, oxbow and stippling
reed-bed, each least bog-seep is gold-
                                tooled script,
is fire-spill from the smelting furnace. Or

say: we see
what the birds see
with their thousand miles to fly
and steering by the flicker-compass
                                in the genes: the stateless
state of water, on the frontier between day and night.

Home, 1990

One day, in that year, and so quietly
that not the closest of us guessed,
    the history of Europe changed.

I don't mean votes and constitutions,
old flags in the attic half a century
    now tentative petals again,

but one day, one night out beyond
the houselights, beside one of those fires
you would tend, and attend,

and chivvy patiently to sleep. (So many
leaves, that year, as if they were pouring in
    on quite another wind.)

It may be some recording angel, veiled
or given momentary body by a furl
    of smoke, might have seen

the moment when, thin blue letter in hand
saying *Come, you can come home now*,
    you knew: the place you'd dreamed

of going back to, with a family,
three horses, a path through the fields,
    was nowhere. *What could I do*

by going, you said later, *except see
it was gone?* Blue paper crinkling in the fire.
Estonia was safe, here, inside you.

Stroke Ward

For those struck
down, in their six beds
as if felled backwards, thunder-
        struck (as you

were, aged six,
bending to a puddle
when a freak of lightning dealt
        a glancing blow)...

For *Boanerges*, sons
of thunder, speechless bearers
of the word, through whom power coursed
        and laid them low

like kings in state,
their boats rigged, flames already
curtaining their longship biers... For
        brothers of the awe-

struck gape,
the awful shark-mouth (you
amongst them, creatures that must work
        the sea, or drown)

sunk now
in some strait between mealtime
and myth... For the conductors, as of lightning,
        each a blown

fuse in the rolling
blackout visible from space
across the continent, one outage after
        another; darkness

floods the bulkheads,
the compartments of the brain...
what words? One man (not you)
    is saying 'Am I

on a course?' (Of study?
Medication? On sealed orders
and a compass bearing?) He says it
    again. And again and again.

In High Care

a high-sided bed
      contains you... not
entirely: these tubes and wires are a part of you too;

that shivery trace,
      you, on the monitor,
the numbers that tot up the oxygen freight in your blood.

The shrink-crumpled black-
      reddish bag of one
transfusion, another of amber like sap from the pine,

not to mention the saline,
      a clear life-tisane –
all you, also hospital property: the conduits and nerves

of its rhythmical-jittery
      self. (Bleeps everywhere,
continual not-quite-always-false alarms.) I lean in;

I'm within the gradual
      devolution of this body,
even less sure than you seem (as you scratch, in a vague

discontent, half-sleeping,
      where sticky-pads itch;
a mosquito has settled, steel proboscis in a vein;

you swat at it) – less sure,
      as I take your hand
to stay it, just at what point *you* begin or end.

Barn Music

Such a long way we've come
        to find ourselves here: us,
                in the ancient instrument.

    (as a small nation's soul
might be plucked on the pulse-strings

of the Internet.) Her fingers

touch-test the *kannel*: part Braille,
        part dowsing – as if voices
                had been buried in the soundbox,

        here crisp, here silky, here
a séance whimper. The sigh-

creak of stroking the length of a string.

Her hands: a weightless skitter now,
        en pointe, across the ballet floor,
                or still, to tease a single

        note out as you might
a splinter from your child's skin.

(I, too, almost have to look away.)

*

Such a long way, maybe centuries,
        to lose ourselves
like this: how the voice, or the flute,
        or cello, sidestep-slip

into each other, or beyond, into clicks
        and pocks, bare bones
of sound, its levers, its machinery
        displayed

(as graceful pale manipulators, black-
    clad against black
drapes, might lay down their marionettes
    to take a bow –

Look, we are nothing, with nothing to hide
    – at the end of their show.)

*

Such a long way to bring us, breathless,
to the borders of pure breath –
breath still audible
just, because
impure

with a trace of *us* in it, our work,
breath-threshers, word-
winnowers, sounds
of our primitive
tools,

the sound-smell of the toil of it, making
/ unmaking ourselves, our bodies
and each other; the hush-
chafe of sweeping
the barn

or the barn burning down, an almost gentle
crackling rush, as the barn-swallow
swoop-staggers out into sky
with smoke behind it,
too late

or early for migration, but it's history;
there's nowhere else to go
but history, and history,
if nothing else,
says *Go…*

kannel: the traditional plucked zither of Estonia, similar to the Finnish *kantele*

Not Quite The Dark Ages

...nor quite the Enlightenment,

more like a small sketched country
     hopefully *developing* –
  the modern and the feudal
leaning on your doorbell side by side

and which is the good news, which

the bad, you have to choose. So:
     1957 – great
   inventions. Like the wheel
scavenged from a buckled pram

that held the tramp's stash in the cutting.

Electricity: an old car battery
     filched from Chris's
    uncle's garage, for
the first experiments on life:

touch Plus and Minus to a worm's

two pinkie-tips and see it thrash and coil.
     Then, broadcasting:
    an army surplus walkie-talkie,
squawk-crackling mouth-piece to ear-piece

like a submariner's last *dive dive dive*

lost in the boom of mid–Atlantic
     murk where Chris's
    never-talked-of dad
might be still struggling to the surface

up a rope ladder of glittering bubbles.

Cargo cults, verging on magic. But this
        was the small state *I* was,
    bluffing for a place
at the conference table, two oil drums

and a plank, in next door's garden shed.

The older boys swapped cigarette cards,
        Players' Navy Cut,
    and strange diplomacies. I
came with a blueprint, inked in rather prettily,

for the atom bomb I was about to test.

The others sniggered, but uneasily.
        I got to slip out at night
    – well, mid-evening; night
would be another country – on mission

to creep twenty gardens to Chris's and back

like a spy, like a sapper, the *maquis*,
        my face as blacked-up
    as I dared – ducking, squeezing
through chinks till… a snag on my sleeve

that I'd fail to explain in the morning

when I flinched at a dog bark somewhere;
        the smell of damp earth
    against my cheek, grit
in my breath, no words for what

I was becoming, what my father

would have shuddered to see: me,
        like a cartoon remake
    of himself, what he'd kept,
he thought, safe,   un-spoken in its own

dark age: a no one, anywhere: a refugee.

Step

Home, after too long
    in hospital, your each
        step hesitant
as if the moment was a shallow stream

to be waded (no
    way round it), maybe
        only inches deep
but too broad, too fast and too loose

with the light,
    its quartzy sand-bed
        patent, magnified,
yet quivering sideways, about to be gone.

Survivor

Is this some reassurance, what the head-scan
reveals: where they live, your nightcomers,

their thin staring children? On a siding
in the bombed-out network of the ageing brain.

They're here tonight again

in the doorway–their wheedling monotone,
affectless scolding, that finger-stab *down*,

down, to send you back, to nail you, a pin
on a map of the front, so sharp that it rips,

East from West, now from then,

and you still wriggling in the gap. Don't fool
yourself, they say, that this *entitles* you, the mere

being, what's the word, *alive*? Bar the doors
if you will. We are here, inside, already.

We have always been here.

Closed Loops

1

No one called today. Nights, that's another story. (What you think is the case, your case, remember. You are liable to be wrong.)

*

Wrong thinking, the head doctor told you. Her smile was kind, but only with her mouth. And you? You don't say. You know what you know.

*

No knowing what the rule book says these days. Serviette or napkin. Britishness? Yours faithfully? Sincerely? Politics at mealtimes is bad form.

*

Form up in lines. He who does not work, neither shall he eat. Nightly, you have your orders. Don't talk back.

*

Back after all these years. *Nyet, nyet.* And then, *Verboten.* Watch your language, you. Caught out, talking to no one.

2

Home visits from the night nurse. Silent, and her two pale, too-pale children watching. One day, she says, all this will be theirs.

*

There's a clause in the lease. Of life. All this can be forfeit. You're a waste of space. A family could live here. You may keep the bed, for now.

*

Now then. (What do the British mean by that?) We have some questions. The guilty know what they are. The innocent (Do you doubt it? Speak up now) have nothing to fear.

*

Fearful whether? said Mrs next door. You wondered what she was driving at. Who knows who knows? From now on, keep your distance.

*

Distance makes the wits go wander. Not far enough. Not, oh, to retrace the tracks, the pale wake on a night sea. To find your way home.

3

Here's another day, apparently. Tick it off on your handwritten roster. Next? (It helps to keep you in the present tense.)

*

Tense times on the borders of sleep. Alarms and ultimatums. You might feel the rumble of a new front, opening (have your bags packed) any time at all.

*

All said and done. The words, three languages or more, worn out. Gone at the elbow. There, the bare, the hunted, animal peeps through.

*

Throughout the night, they scour the flat. The fridge. They have the key, and hunger, and we all have secrets. They know which.

*

Which *would* you spend your time with, after all – vague mouthing blurs, like me? Or faces, sharp even in darkness, voices never too whispered to hear?

4

Tales, fairy tales of reason. *Whereof we cannot speak, thereof...* But mind abhors a silence. There is something more than *everything that is the case.*

*

Case study? *Life* study. Or *lives.* Ones you lost (your own and others). Ones the slightest choice or chance could have written down to your account.

*

Count days. Time jolts, to someone else's say-so. British Summer/ Greenwich Mean. Last week, you missed a beat, and lived two days outside our time.

*

Time was, you'd have known what to do. Now, your voice gone thin and child-like, for me to decide. Heavy as lead, that feather in the scales called Will.

*

Will the voices come tonight? Yes. Through the air-vent, hissing. Closed loops, snakes of accusation. Just try to remember: they are eating their own tails.

5

Life is TV, untuned. Mainly interference. And TV itself? Grins. Gunshots. Lust at all hours. What's the sense? Laughter, at anything, from nowhere.

*

Know where you live. The Prime Minister. Day of the week. This isn't paranoia: get caught out, you could be held against your will.

*

Will anything appease them, the nightcomers? Small gifts, in brown paper? Could you just surrender? Say Enough, enough? As if it was that simple.

*

Simple and nodding, your grandmother sat. Nodding. Maybe she knew something, in her vacancy. (*Anything*, you once promised yourself, *but come to this*.)

*

This, this is the judgment of the heart. *Enough?* you say to it. But it's implacable. Beats on. The sentence: life, life, life.

Flat Earthers

Flat earth: how
could they have thought it?
Where did they imagine that the sail

they watched diminish to a crisp horizon
might sink and yet sometimes
return? And what
could he be seeing,
waving from his doorstep,
one hand shielding his eyes, one raised

as if I was that sail, or more workaday
funnel (ferry or freighter, maybe
the last boat out)
that's gone
all but its smear on the haze?
Diminishment. You'd think it was the air

not his eyes fogging over – wipe, try
to wipe it with a wave, as I drop
not out of sight
but out
of question. I'm already
hypothetical, like the rattling loose-

change data we have to dismiss
from the edge of a world-
view for fear
the globe
slips off its spindle.
Squinting into his gaze, I see myself

become a visitation, the kind
known by the vague
cool space
    it leaves behind it,
  as empty and charged
with a flavour, a heft, as the place

in which another word that he *had*
yesterday persists
in being,
    almost ruthlessly

The Works

...and what did the store room contain
once it was empty?
              Beyond dust,

something scorched, a tyre-burn, half metallic,
on the smell-horizon; and

the silence of downed tools – be exact:
that of particular names
                          (*gear hobber,*

core or ribbon blender), true names
someone would have known

as if by nature (*pre-cured tread press, cold
feed extruder*)
        like the snug in the palm

of a lever or grip (*dispersal kneader,
pelletiser*), metal warming to the hand

that used it. No generic silence, this,
but particular gaps
                      in the air, the way

the absences of *hardy, top fuller, slack
tub* linger in specific corners

of a converted smithy, or this and that
endearment
        (*add your own*

        here if you have them) in the language
of a worn-out love.

Variations on a Theme from the Cornish

An lavar coth yu lavar gwîr
Bedh darn nêver, dhan tavaz rê hîr
Mez dên neb dawaz a gallaz i dîr.
The old saying is a true saying
Never will good come from a tongue too long
But a man without a tongue shall lose his land.

CORNISH PROVERB

The man without a tongue will lose his land
Or: one who's lost his land will hear his tongue

grow stranger than the speech he moves among.
The land where loss is dumb will lose the man

and gain a stranger, and the stranger's song
will shift where few and fewer understand

lost to itself. The tongue without a man
will make a land of dumbness, that no one

who learns its lexicon can leave again,
its rivers swollen with unspoken wrong

and all the bridges down. Belong, be long:
the last words. They revert to wind.

A stone slip on the wet scree. Rain.
A lost thing at the door. A gift of tongues.

Fall

You catch yourself;
I've caught you in that moment –
in the Richter-scale

order of things, a mere

blip: a synapse blinks, you jolt,
a fault line gives and
                                    it catches itself

like a step off the kerb edge of sleep,

the startle reflex newborns come with.
                                    (*Bang!*
you mime it, later, though the words

have gone.) At ninety-one

life is a falling sickness,
visitation
of the heavy gods. *Come on,*

come down.

Last week
I turned away while you were dressing, and
Bang! you were cheek to carpet

at ninety degrees to the world in which I am

for now – your eyes wide, as if
listening, as if the earth had spoken
so (in your deafness, at last)

you could hear it. *Come home.*

Birch, His Book

In the hospital garden

where few things and fewer
each day answer to their names

they meet – man,
tree. Both are deciduous.

They greet each other
formally, by touch.

Look, birch,

I can't help saying
like a ripple back

and up through generations,
how each of us learned

(*look Jake* (*look Jonathan*
(*look Philip* (*look*

))   )   )

that in whoever's garden,
wilderwood or waste,

wherever we
stand one to one with one,

of all trees this
requires

to be addressed:

*

birch. As if a word

(which he can't hear)
might be a clearing

in a clearing in the centuries-
dark forest's crowd-interior,

just wide enough for one
tree to draw down the light,

as if he might step through,

he peels a strip
of damaged white

curling back like planed shavings
and the underside

is the rust-purple not-
quite-night glow-shadow

like the moon in full eclipse.

He squints as if uncertain
what if anything

he's reading,
whether it's a trick

of time or failing sight.
It's no use asking him.

I have to look.

Nimzo-Indian

Now that all other bearings have led him, astray,
       to the last but one ward, now
that even the en-suite bathroom keeps eluding him

like socks or what he started out for from his chair

or family faces, which of us might come in
          wearing whose, from when,
now what can I do but... *here* : the foursquare

board, the rattling-out of chessmen. He looks up.
I set him out white that's gone amber with touch

and he's playing a stout Nimzo-Indian, six
          moves or more ahead, away
from this new-scrubbed room with fragments of him

on one shelf. His lips moving. Under his breath,

the cut-glass combinations on a waiter's silver tray
          of poise and tremor, upheld,
tinkling, nothing spilled yet but angles of light...

When he slips – yes, his fingertips dither then
go to my knight, not his own – it's the highest mistake

such as God might have made: to reach so deep
          into world that (maybe this
is what He longed for) He forgot Himself in it.

Spoor

Eurostar, Cardiff–Amsterdam

1

Doctor doctor
it's the way things pour

on round me when I shut my eyes

like the glassy but shuddering pause
at the lip of the weir.

It's either that

or the stasis of speed,
the way the furthest tree keeps pace

unmoving, while what's near

(tell me: is this a sign
of ageing? or the age?)

twitches past in a blur.

2

And now: I'm in the dark
of tunnel vision.

How much of the journey will be
in non-space, new space
borrowed from the earth or sea

or from the air above a valley?

Here's a flicker, in the long
view, of a granite viaduct's brief

being-there-ness – and me

one pulse in that flicker. Crack
an atom, track its scattered spores
of particles; you have to choose

which to grasp: mass or velocity.

Is that the bargain, then: the more
we're everywhere,

the less substantial we will be?

   3

And now: looking down into gardens,
          which could be yours
or anyone's, though more likely
            the poor...
Their bedrooms even, each unguarded
               detail magnified
like mist-intricate rockpool weed.
          (The child
I was reached in to touch, and missed
as my arm became crooked, the hand
      not quite mine;
it could have turned to me
    and beckoned;
it had crossed the line.)

   4

Faced backwards, I'm ready to fall
into my destination unforewarned

except there's this shadow, not unlike my own

thrown by its, no, by many lights
behind me, into fragments, a diaspora,

displacements, which however come in, on

and clearer if I step towards them,
draw them closer to the vanishing point

where they will, no, *we* will, be one.

5

As in the station washroom,
my reflection in grey polished steel,

the see-and-see-through self
advancing in the automatic door

before the stomach-punch thud
and wheeze of opening... so

yesterday, his vague
shape through the falling-water blur

of language, through ninety years,

he came shuffling

towards me, head
shaved as if for delousing,

on the (tactfully) locked ward?

6

Now I'm out of my languages (English,
French) and on the crowded
InterCity through Den Haag,

the shape of space around me changed,

between me and the next man, and
the next, by the lack of one casual word
we might share; it recalls me

to the cramped airless world of the shy

... to him, in his word-naked
world, as tight as a lift cage,
strangers pressing in too close

and some of them in uniform

... or to any illegal, without papers,
the air sweating against him,
every breath a risk. Do not meet

word with word, or eye with eye.

7

Of course things *pour*.
You want a different planet?

Right now, we're sitting here faster
than the speed of sound.

The wonder is that we can talk,
I mean, *converse*, at all.

8

Did I think I was going to meet him
half way – after-image at least,

the inside-out of what his converse
journey must have printed on his eye,

all his kind, coming out of the east /
west rip of Europe (1946,

that was, already hardening
like a bad scar)

truck-loaded through wrecked
Rhinelands, fallen sky

for miles in flood-fields
where the dykes were breached

– *Europe After The Rain*
as in Ernst's wax-rubbing, not

of a plaque or tomb but the hide
of one predator reptile or other

that had thrashed and gored and
thrashed before they (he

could never quite believe it)
died?

9

Where
in his brain
between the dried

blood shadow
of stroke damage,
doctor

doctor, are
the traces?
Scuff marks

in the dust. A stray
print in the mud.
Where can I track

(I find a word
in Dutch now on the station
indicator board

for track as in railway,
for these lines)
his *spoor*?

How We Knew

you were leaving: when the sweet
hey-ho of that first glee
song of a new June day

didn't lift you from your chair;

when a walk in the care home's
courtyard square
was a headlong slow trudge

like sledge-hauling in a blizzard

making for the Pole; when a pinch
of herb – lavender,
duskdusty rosemary –

between my fingers made you flinch

as if it might divert you
from your hurry
to get nowhere; as if

nowhere itself might not wait.

The Scarecrow

you swapped clothes with,
its rags for the wrong side's fatigues,
in an Austrian field, as a war
that's history to me

collapsed in on itself, who knows
how many buried,

gave you life.
You always meant to go back
nine hundred miles, so many years,
say thank you,

maybe learn its name. Too late now.
You can spare yourself the journey;

it's here
tinder-light: twig-fingers,
hollowed sockets, wind sounds
in its cavities

in this hospital cot
in your place.

Finally

the body animal, still strong,
stronger than sense
or wanting,
writhing in the trap.

As if it, his own person, is the snare
that bites still, and more sharply
the harder he strains,
at every point.

Not just Odin
on the world tree, or any other
of your hanged gods.
Just say any human,

any you or me or no one
in the ranks,
poor bloody infantry,
left hanging on the old barbed wire.

Seep

1

A small bird up, *tseep*
tseep, and at it as the first
light leaks in round the blinds:
all the wincing precision
      of a wonky wheel.
We're getting somewhere, says
        the fond machine.

2

No wonder, say my joints,
my gristle, that we ache.
      It's salty water seeping
inwards. There's enough to be done
      without the excess baggage
      of a word like 'tears'.
On we go, rusting slowly.

3

It's the being near, too
near him, as the substance
      of him seeps away.
Topsoil from bedrock. Breath
      from leaky airlock, to
the vacuum – having done its job
      relaxing, into space?

4

      Then again. Do we think it's only
      one way, entropy?
Sense it now, in the garden, something

too diffuse to guard against, cool and not
        quite a scent in the air: June
morning entering, tentatively, not pushy
        like summer too surely arrived.

5

He's thinning himself down, for one
        more border he must slip across.
                Out, to… We want a choice
of word like 'spirit' here. We look that way
        and he evades us, slipping deeper in
the body. Moist thing. Humus. Itch,
        hunger, toothache, that is what he is.

6

                Into the body, and out –
he no longer contains himself
exactly. Swabbing and flushing away
        we might be missing something:
        what we want to keep is a husk.
He is down and away in his constituents,
        into the world's. Down the drain.

7

And we're wrong-footed, surely
        as in the other story
where they're in the garden (dust
        still cool from night; now,
a bird.) They look the wrong way
        asking no one in particular
                who moved the stone.

Point

       : as when the black-
bird is so still
   that it becomes a black
bird-shaped gap between the lit
leaves, like the song of its own

      unsinging; as a cat
resolves to black, pure cat-
   shaped hole in the world,
maybe watching the bird, and
you too watching, void of form

      and voice. Distil
it to a point, the sudden
   night sky you
step out of the back door into
and it takes your breath away.

Later

after the work stopped
      water filled the quarry pit
(just a kerb of raw pink limestone showing
by the cherry-ripe DANGER DEEP WATER sign)
         then it was available for light

and for transients, drawn
      by its glint from the sky.
The landscaped car park bays are emptying
in the all-at-once late afternoon, a safely-gathered-in
         of scattered child cries for the night.

A small flock (black
      snags I can't name
in a reflected satin blue) is intent on itself,
its scoots, squabbles and lulls, as busy as a shopfloor
         at being the species they are

dip-and-shrugging and
      frisking themselves. One
stands up, almost, on the water, up-and-un-
ruffling wings of spray like (from here, with low sun
         behind) those of a larger

brighter bird than itself
      which is also itself
extended into space around it, the sensible
world. *Itself...* Yes, maybe that's what *self* is, not
         a tight-inside-us nub

but what we are, thrown
      out and off, un-self-seen,
once-for-all, betraying even as it leaves us
our position, giving itself (don't you long
         to say 'gladly'?) away

Glosa: *Westron Wynde*

Westron wynde, when will thou blow
The small rains down can rain
Cryste, if my love was in my armes
And I in my bedde again!

ANON, MEDIEVAL

Where were we? Something shifted in the night,
as if the house resettled – ground
easing itself with a groan... If not
the house, then maybe weather. The wind
still held its... not quite a note,
rather, a space into which a note might go,
live and not matter, like the sound of sand
that travellers' tales called *singing*. Infinite
distance but close, like that nobody's song: *oh*
westron wynde, when will thou blow...

Where are you now, who couldn't hold a tune
or the country of singers you left? You'd no choice
about that, any more than for me, my tone-
deaf smudges on the air that no advice,
no scolding at the age of ten
could school. No choice but *play it again*,
for us both, that shared halt in the voice
on the phone or off guard. It's my turn
to hear its crackle at the windowpane:
The small rains down can rain.

That's not your language or your kind of song,
or not in public. *Tears, idle tears...*?
Give me patience! you'd say. Give tongue
to rage, grief or repining, they take liberties,
and homes, and lives. One must be strong.
You were – outliving friends and false alarms,
heart pills and hospital calls, for thirty years,
eventually alone... where you seemed to belong,
not free from but at home with harm.
Crsyte, if my love was in my armes

though who or what your *love* might signify,
buried in languages she could not speak,
my mother soon learned not to pry.
A wind from somewhere colder, it might leak
through the cracks in your voice, as now in mine.
Leave it to music, then to silence, to explain
what words would make too rigid and too weak.
The wind has shifted; so we redefine
our foursquare walls by what they can't contain.
You, gone. And I... *I in my bedde again.*

Jacob's Island

A little battered, lightly
drubbed and keelhauled,
washed over the reef,

but peaceful –
stretched out, sleeping
with some sort of smile:

some sort of sailor,
shipwrecked, washed by chance
or grace ashore.

What land is this?

Can't say – on our far coast
we barely heard the breakers – but
in ways we can't guess,

in the small hours,
without knowing,
we have all been changed.

The maps will have to be redrawn.

Terra Incognita – write it

here. Beneath our feet.

Legacy

Willed, to you

my children, any stock or bond might weaken,
any trust decay, like anything in man's
estate. And then

there's *you*, how you stand – attention
elsewhere, a half tense half delicate slouch,
provisional

as if standing on hold. In silhouette or kindly
light you might be taken for my, my for your,
reflection. Then again

there's *you* – repeating what I said between
two frayed ends of a moment twenty years ago
which I forget...

Some unwilled thing. Somewhere too far
or near to see, feel the rippling lift into flight: birds
on their centuries'

migration, out of the distance in us (we're
a resting place, a night stop), out of our far-north
ancestors, and gone

into the dark of our descendants, through
that space called *me* at one time,
at another, *you* or *you*.

Hrmsa

: a word, that's barely
on the edge of sense, or senses:
h... r... m... s...

four consonants, each with the force
of a vowel, with its own voice, self-

sufficient in a way our English won't permit

but can't forbid. Survivor
in stray place names, that clings like the smell
of wild garlic, of *ramsons* – those fresh-

out-of-nowhere cool green flames
through the leaf litter in a moist wood.

Then the flower-froth, milk boiling over

into tang, clean appetite.
A few weeks on and it's collapsing,
liquefying into stink

determinedly, more willed than withering,
pale bulbs sucking their life back

under. Come summer, it's gone.

*

A word clearing its throat, word
on the edge of human. What comes next
might be snuffle or roar

because this is *alium ursinum*, bear-garlic
truffled up by European brown bear

and wild boar – word gone to ground,

with a taste of extinction. So what
has been scrumpling the undergrowth, here,
at the end of the street, or who? A word

with the smell of it on them, on the breath
(the word breathes heavy), like an accent

souring your vowels from twelve hundred years ago?

*

A word that's away, off, shambling into cover
in this deep moist crease, too steep for use, let
go, of wild-wood, fly-tipped and intractable,

where things slip down the seam
between park and track and gardens, where

he's out too late – he should be home

by now – lost in the smell of garlic and its pale
glow rising, old man with his bear-gait, quiet
berserker, bear-pelt-wearer, out

of our element, who can place
by taste, by touch, wood sorrel, soursabs,

ramsons in their season, though their names

elude him now. He wanders.
For a word that's lost
its voice, a voice

that is losing its words…
The dusk of language. Night-

cries – listen – barely human to our ears.

Bark Moth

and sometimes for an instant

just to see
unseen,

dusty bark-patterned moth,
antennae scanning

– to wear

the veil of here-
and-elsewhere,

eyes at the dark slit
of their own choice

– to pass among

crowds, thickets of sensation
without rustling a leaf

– to be no named thing

that would stand between
light and the light that answers

      grass blade – *present*
      dried leaf – *present*
      sweet wrapper boot print copper beetle –
      present present present equally

and no shadow
cast in my shape on the world

Phlogiston

1

How does fire do it – prop
the ladder of itself against the air,
      then climb it?
I must study this, in passing.

2

A thin
twig in the embers
flexes, as if waking.
It fills from the inside
as with sap, with the burning.
You could almost believe it: Fire
is a kind of life; life is a kind of fire.

3

We call it hungry, call it
                wild – what swings
from branch to branch tip of the spitting
eucalyptus
      or drops
on all fours in the brushwood
snuffling up the in-draught of a hunger –
                        oxygen.
The drunk kids scatter, shrieking with half-laughter.
No stopping it now
          or them ever
             or us,
sucked in, though we call it breaking
         news, call it consuming
             curiosity.

4

No wonder we talk about *playing*
hose-jets on the conflagration.
                              Fire
and water recognise each other
from way back, a shared childhood.
        Is this dancing?
See them rush into each other's arms.

5

Fire is in the past tense
when the bright flags break out
like a victory parade
                        decreed.
The flame is already an *after*.
Blindfold, in the unmarked cell
or cellar, history, the deed
of fire is already done.

6

Just as the paper gives in to weightless
            dissolution, see the ink's
fusewire-thin tangle hanging
        in the blaze, intact,
                    as if her parting
message had been written on the flame.

7

Buddha's sermon
spoke about a house on fire.
Fire's own homily runs on this
one thing: its escape
from the house of the earth.

8
Flames:
          doors
thrown open, the guests
          spilling out already
                    with their heedless laughter
from the banquet, filled
          and never
fulfilled, where the carriages
          are waiting, black
                    coach horses stamping;
off then, clattering,
their far
          spark only deepening
                    the night.

9
In the end these
tongues I trust

will speak me
perfectly.

Nothing lost in the translation.

Dirac: The Tower

The heart of the matter,
it seems, is silence. And we seem to need them,
these saints of the strange –
how they seem to know something

of which even their equations are a shadow-play.
To *picture* it would be
'like a blind man touching a snowflake'

but try: fractal-layered as that snowflake, blush-lit
like picturehouse drapes
for us who love our colours, who'd see
in the pure equations only intersecting angles

of transparency,
the heart of matter – like a tower,
for all the world like Babel except

meant. 'The smallest imaginable number of words
that someone with the power of speech
could utter in company
per hour = 1 *dirac.*' Towers

of silence – earth's fond tongues unpeeling,
as deciduous as autumn, in itself
a kind of Fall

into knowledge. If there's a language up there,
at the vanishing point of summit,
it's that of... could they be
angels, without footing on the earth

or friendship? And let's not pretend it's kindness
has them part the clouds (sometimes)
to open a crack

in matter through which who knows what might come
into the world, to blind us.
They have to be strange
enough themselves to breathe that thin cold air

a little, not enough
to bring back words that we could follow
even had we ears to hear.

Theoretical physicist Paul Dirac (1902-84) was famous for his taciturnity and
precision. The first quote here was said by, the second of, him. A sculpture
by Simon Thomas contributes to this poem.

The Garden of Nebamun

(tomb painting, Egypt, c. 1400 BC)

Almost too much, the bounty:

palm and fig tree glowing,
lit by hanging-lanterns of ripe fruit;

jars, baskets filled for a feast,
a journey; great fish in the lotus pool

with their jaws hanging open,
here where hunger cannot be.

No need for it, no need.

Dried, preserved beyond hope
of decay, these grapes and dates

have outlived all conceivable harvests,
all known colours wearing thin,

all tones tending towards sandy
as the desert rises through the carpet,

all the outside coming in, in

like a dry tide, like the weariness of life
eternal, and the edges of the picture

flake away. It's an island of faded delight,
a detail near the edge of Mappa Mundi

towards which we might strive
forever and where – if the gods are truly

bountiful – we need never arrive.

Suncatcher

World of Conservatories. Welcome. I don't see
                a way in, or out.
But here are four, together, as snug a ménage
                as the compass rose,
leading each off the others.

This arch, a Gothic touch, a bevelling or not
                of panes, a word
like *mullion* or *gazebo* spoken in the same
                RP of PVC.
a hint of greenhouse palaces

at Kew, here; there, a Bauhaus glass equation,
                a machine
for growing old in... Antechamber of the afterlife.
                (It's up to you,
for we have *choice*,

to say if this is Heaven.) And the light, the light
                to which they turn
is yearning – *leisure* – endlessly refracted.
                Freed at last, freed
from the gravity of everyday,

spun into orbit, they revolve around each other,
                like suncatcher vanes
of a space station, their voltaic cells, pale souls,
                stretching out for the tan
the gaze of God might give.

Slow waltzer in the soundless fairground,
                you could turn it
like a crystal vase. Glints in the bevels.
                You're the face, maybe,
they leap to their feet

from their loungers to point at, awestruck
                as at an eclipse,
though then again who are you but a huge
                reflection of themselves,
or their own absence, looking in?

Tuonela

(after Sibelius)

No, it's not as I thought, that we move
and it (grey water harder than
the whaleback granite round it, ice-
raked out of the north) is still.

#

But the swan's imperceptible
way of having glided, though it seemed a pale-
etched shape in glass with dark behind it...
this is what unnerves.

#

From the train now, rush-hour stasis:
late October morning, light enough
for a shuffling of greys, enough dark
still for lights on: Tuonela

#

in the city; Western Avenue
gives a ripple of brake lights, bright-dim
like an impulse down the neurons –
daily, we are all- and inter-changed

#

like music. How many times
to the same shore, same score
conducted by Järvi or Salonen, same
notes in a different wind across the water? Cry

#

of wild geese, late this season. I
can do this with headphones
or I close my eyes, where it's never
quite dark, even night slightly prickling

#

no stars on that lake; the glints that run
to, through each other
on its surface might be ours reflected
if I could hold still enough to see

#

the point where endless
movement finally amounts to stillness: Tuonela
isn't elsewhere, it's not even *after*
(I could call on the dead here:

#

bear me out – yes, you
who've stepped out of the singular
of your self and your self and yet resist the plural;
I can't focus on you or on you

#

– your unsettlement contained
by distances come close, tideless water
without features to distinguish one
shore from the other). As I change

#

trains as I wait for my connection
sudden lit windows flicker between this
and an opposite platform now
a crowd, now empty when I look again:

#

Tuonela. It was meant to be grey
or less, no colour, and cold
to numbness. It was meant to be between
now and never. Tuonela is here, is a way

#

to hold our so much, so many, our
so mattering: a gaze such as implies
an eye, black and returning no expression to us,
that implies a swan.

Dummies

We've caught them at their ease,

maybe even at play.
Round the back of the Medical School,

eavesdroppers through the window,
we don't see much good of ourselves.
There's a couple of plastic half-men

cross-sectioned like pigs on the hook
in the butcher's back room.

That torso might, if she had hands,

have been peeling the flaps back
like ripe fruit, into her ventral cavity

to show us something deeper
than a sacred heart. That leg,
that flexed wrist, might be spare

odd parts of any body there,
kicked off like outdoor shoes.

They're as raw as a burn

but bloodless: simulations, hobby-kits
of organs with a shrink-wrapped look,

the family jewels in paste, veins plump
and bonny, not a bit like death
– like life, maybe,

if we were between incarnations,
shoppers at the Spring Sale window,

pinched and peeking, outside in the cold.

Mist over the Weir

that must work at it, work at it
turning river into spray,

into this; mist factory, the mist
that's needed to conceal the workings

of the world, the gravity
machine, that makes itself

in dogged rapt self-meditation,
cloudy, for the making's sake.

*

This drift back up, and over,
      like a, or *is* it a,
memory: that particular chill
         on the skin
and in the membranes of the nose –
                not quite a smell,

slight coldness coexisting with whatever
      temperature around it?
Condensation. Sublimation.
        Mystery
and physics: energy ingested
           by a change

like that ghost story trope:
      the body's shape
in coldness, how it seems to feed
         on the warmth in the air
in our flesh, in the process
           between state and state.

*

The water, coming to its frayed edge, tries
to be two things: both the mirror

and the misting that means *not
yet ended*, held to its own lips.

Barry Island, with Dante and Ducks

In the here- and the anywhere-after
        of the funfair, they're
bobbing, they're jostling,
        as snub-nosed and up-for-it
                as ocean-going tugs

yolk-yellow shallow-draughted
        plastic ducks. Poor
souls. Or not whole souls but
        appetites; they nudge

                in a slow spin, the slew
of the circular stream – say it:
        Dante, with cheerier music –

while glum baffled kids stare in,
        wanting, certainly wanting,

                uncertainly sure just what.

But we'll give it a whirl,
        a quid a go,

with bamboo fishing sticks.
        They're surprisingly coy,
                these ducks; their cup-hooks

begging like the Brahmacharya's Śikhā,
        his god-handle tuft
(just one hair is enough,
        one flick, to winch us up

                out of the world of illusion)
for the click
        with a copper curtain ring
on a chain, the quiver-tip
        of her six-year-old's slim concentration

(and grandfather helping –
is it helping that I do?)
They bump, spin, mutely
dodgem, but yes,

between us, one's hooked.
She comes home
with a neon-green flubbery monkey.

already with a look of Was
that *it?* We paid over the odds,

but who said they were even,

or even the point?
The point

is that we buckled to it, me
with stiff knees, kneeling almost,
at her side, till we met

at the point of pure
attention,
the vanishing point,
a kind of ever-after

in the here and Thursday,
with the smell of burgers
beach tar, spindrift pink
of candyfloss, a bit
of grace, a bit of luck.

Goal

One flash and no looking back, that
        moment, soundless,
through the plate-glass frontage
of the big-screen *(Catch The Big Game*
            BIGGER!) bar: some

goal! has lifted them clean off their bar stools
        and out of themselves,
their mouths wide, like one full-on
gust of wind; there may be words
            and, somewhere, losers

(in some mirror-image bar) but here,
        now, he's untouchable –
one lad in the dozen, a tad doughy
where his team strip top rides up, but hey,
            a good half-metre skyward

as if hoisted by his high-flung fists –
        Ye-e-es! – launched
like a toddler from a rough grip
under armpits, as if gravity had shrugged
            and dad's glasspaper grin

could be always below, great laughter
        like God's, without words
in any language, without rights or wrongs
or sides to fall back into. Why else
            can we dream of flying,

unless we were made for this?

Whit

We draw these grids,
can't help it, even
on the sky:
the sheer
mirror-wall block
by Queen Street station,
fine-ruled into rentable
units, and barely
a whit
of difference
between it and sky,
this near-dusk that's white-
green and watery clear
till... a what?
a speck,
a singularity,
comes into being
at the unseen seam, a gull-
silhouette, that flies out
of itself, in two
directions,
a creation
suddenly *ab nihilo*:
Bede's sparrow for a quantum world,
a cracked particle shied,
neutrons spinning
awry, leaving
their fossil-
fern-frond traces
of decay; each of the both of it
symmetrically swerves
(I'm not making
this up;
light
strikes the glass
and optic nerve just so)

and re-enters itself,
　　and is nothing
　　　(or nothing
　　　　　that the wit
　　　　　of man can grasp)
　　　　　　　　again

Words for the Shortest Day

the turn: its stripped-
down late

December light
shed equally

on what's best let go, what
comes round again

e.g. the word
'again'

once
and again

*

the word 'once'

now there's
a mystery...

how many times
do I have to repeat it

before it dares to stand alone?

*

those insatiable
ascetics
gorging on denial

(this should be their festival
if anyone's)

till barely a clock-
tick separates
their 'less' from 'more'

*

'barely'
    'hardly'
        'scarcely' :
three words come in

as if out of medieval weather

landscape simplified to black and white
by snow, each stone hedge
its own shadow:

almost uninhabitable
clarity of the only-just-
enough... and yet

think of Mother Julian's
Creator's palm,
holding out and up

(forever)
this small brittle nut

and it was everything

*

and everything
the mystery (I re-
capitulate):
        'once'
and
    'forever'
and
           'again'

Epiphany Weather

Don't be afraid; it *is* fearful,
     what the out-there, the out-in-the-cold,

wants – what it whirls at us,
     its fast thick flurries in the air,

against the pane. Like life
     arriving when least asked for. Undecided

between rain, sleet, sleet and snow,
     the gusts come, sharp as bad intent

or love. We flinch. And we open the door.

     There, where its sudden glow hits night,
they're closer than we'd guessed, these

     no-bodied shapes. Tricks of our light,
cold sparks of detail pouring through them

     out of and into the dark, they stand
as if astonished by the fact of us,

     a few specks melting on the threshold
like an offering for the child.

Snow the Cartographer

has pored all night
over the finer details
of the hill beyond the city.

Each fence and hedge has awoken today

to its responsibility:
define, define and demarcate
– the bare cold facts abstracted

from the sensual give and take

of shape and shade: a Land Registry
of plans, to do with holdings,
which it's up to us to colour-by-numbers

in with *theirs*, *ours*, *you* and *me*.

And snow? It's already away, with other
plans to draw up, off and ever back
to tundra, a time without edges, snow-

sleep blowing, settling, constantly,

where everything hunkers
and the snow itself is puzzled, piqued
to find like a niggling dream

the tracks of a lone

band of a skin-clad species
drawn to the extremities
of the liveable world, even there

to pitch camp – dare to call it *home*.

Some People Have Communications

with the dead. This, from you,

John, and no,
you haven't recovered the power of speech

or found a way of living on in time to now.

It's in the back-then you are, in the time
you had forgotten

time – but it's always

one moment: you've turned
at a touch of the sun, and stand

as if you might not move again

as I did just now between platforms,
between trains: I stopped, was stopped

as sure as if someone had spoken my name.

Which they'd not. Nor had you.
But I turned in a direction, out

of shadow, eyes

closed, simple instinct
angling, the way a late-

in-the-season butterfly (I see

a tattered Tortioseshell) will shift
and quiver into mute alignment.

You'd have noticed that too.

Orrery

Unwrap it how you will,
peeling clouds and angels, star-
patterned tissue-paper, down to bare
brass bones, this seems to be it:
      the jerk-tick of a clockwork orrery,

God's train set in the dark room,
left to run down, glinting now and then
if anyone was there to see.
The astrolabe with its farthingale
      hoops. The armillary sphere.

In Joseph Wright of Derby's
chiaroscuro-drenched *A Philosopher
Lecturing on the Orrery*
two children lean and stare
      not at him, the master

(who anyway looks elsewhere;
posterity is already listening,
he thinks) but into the heart
of things, be it only a candle.
      Unwrap the mathematics how you will

from this once-in-a-life conjunction
of wandering stars; peel off the words
like *father*, *son*, and wider orbits,
great- and *grand-*, beyond
      and we know those two children are right:

not speaking, side by side and gazing
into what the painter can't paint –
drawn to, till they almost are,
      the source of light.

White Night

North: not only the five-month winters'
snow and ice, but this

at the opposite end of the seasons:
the reflection of their whiteness,

blue-white, green-white, night-white,
in midsummer sky.

even the bonfire burning palely,
birch trunks giving up their whiteness to the flames.

*

*Who might you be
if you weren't who you are tonight?*
: a question that makes sense

on a night beyond-weary, beyond-
partied, beyond-drunk, as if we had come

together on an uninhabited low island
not always glimpsed from the shore,

beyond us, westward, tideless sea,

*

the time he held on for through his sad Novembers
as if exiled half the year.
                                    I knew he was away

when he stared at the words on the page
I'd felt-penned, child-like:

MIDSUMMER EVE TONIGHT

as if he was staring straight through, out some other side

*

we neither believed in. Sleepless,
wakeless now, tonight, it's me

at four a.m., after days
of yawning at all hours,

sheet pulled over my eyes, and still
these northern lights, this bluish

glimmer on my retina,
his white night in my brain.

*

North sky, the night when night
and day sit down together until dawn

suffused with… not claret, but maybe
birch sap, not blood but

let's consider lymph: who knew,
through most of history, we had this clear

companion to the red and thumping stuff
of which we told so many stories?

*

North, and *who*

> *might you be*

after winter, that sharpens our edges,
makes us more distinct,

if you weren't who you are?
Mild now, after the blaze and leaping,

in a clearing in the forest or the sea

(some of the drowned are also here)

*

in the wide, widening circle

we could melt into the distance

and distance itself
sits in among us, guest

we can't count,
> kind

wolf in from the horizon

all forgiven now, or soon

* Jaaniõhtu: (Estonia) the Midsummer festival, the eve of St John's Day.